Threads & Fri[ends]
BOOK SEVEN

Gary the Third Baseman Learns Hard Work

by Peter J. Mulry

Copyright © 2021 Peter J. Mulry. All rights reserved. Except for brief quotations for review purposes, no part of this book may be reproduced in any form without prior written permission from the author.

Published by:
Peter J Mulry Foundation

Contact the author:
peterjmulryfoundation.org
850-221-1045

Print - ISBN: 978-1-7358638-6-3

I would like to thank several people who made this book possible - Lou Maggio, KR Lombardia, Gary Ippolito and Andy Taylor. I would also like to thank Mario Garcia, my Guardian Angel who has been with me through this endeavor. A tip of the cap to all the sponsors for their financial support.

Thanks to all who have helped me on my journey.

On a sunny, warm day, the All Stars gathered in the dugout before their first game of the new season. Gary the Third Baseman took a seat on the bench in the back and fiddled with his glove. "Let's make this our best season yet!" Coach Threads said to his players. "I'm sure you all worked hard in the off-season so that you'd be ready for our first game. Now let's get out there and beat the Wildcats!"

The team cheered and hurried out to the field. Gary plodded over to his place behind third base. He'd stayed up late last night watching a television show with his sister, and he was tired. He yawned while he waited for the game to start. After Coach's speech, Gary felt a little guilty for not practicing like the others had, but he was sure he would be able to field the ball just as well today as he had last season.

The Wildcats' first batter stepped up, Pedro pitched the ball, and the batter swung too high, missing the ball. "Strike One!" called the umpire.

On the second pitch, the bat made a hard crack, and sent the ball in Gary's direction. He stumbled as he ran back, but caught it at the last moment, and threw it toward Freddy on first base. Gary's throw went wide, and Freddy couldn't reach the ball in time to stop the batter from crossing first base. The batter stopped on second and gave Gary a grin.

The whole game, Gary struggled to catch the ball whenever it went in his direction. A ground ball rolled past him, then he fumbled the catch when Sam threw him the ball to tag a runner coming past third base. A little while later, the All Stars lost to the Wildcats, 5-1. The All Stars left the field, feeling a little down because they'd started their new season with a loss.

Coach Threads came up to Gary. "Everything okay? You seemed to be missing a lot of catches today."

"I'm just having a bad day," Gary said. He didn't want to tell Coach that he hadn't practiced much during the off season. He'd played video games, gone swimming, and hung out with his friends instead of practicing. After all, he'd been on the team for two years now and was a good player, at least most of the time.

"I'm going to schedule some extra practices on Tuesdays and Thursdays," Coach Threads said. "I think it would be a good idea if you came."

Gary didn't want to go to extra practices. He had lots of other fun things he wanted to do instead. "Thanks, Coach," he said. "But I'm pretty busy."

"You don't just let the team down when you don't practice," Coach Threads said. "You let yourself down, too. You're a great third baseman, Gary, and if you work a little harder, you can be an excellent third baseman."

TUESDAY

THURSDAY

All weekend, Gary thought about what Coach Threads had said. But when Tuesday came around, Gary went home instead of going to the extra practice. On Thursday, he made plans to get ice cream with a friend instead of going to the extra practice.

When he showed up on the field Saturday for their next game, Gary saw most of the team was already there, practicing before the game. Coach Threads was running drills, with Cathy the Catcher throwing the ball to Sam the Second Baseman, who would then throw to Louie in left field, or to Rita in right field. Each time, the players made the throw a little faster than the time before. "Great job!" Pedro the Pitcher said, while the rest of the team cheered.

They all sure looked like they were having fun even though they were working hard, Gary thought. Everyone's throws were perfect, and no one fumbled the ball like he had at the game last week.

"Gary!" Louie called out. "Come on over and practice with us!"

"Maybe next time," Gary said. He was sure that first game had just been a bad day. But as the second game of the season got underway, he missed more throws and catches, and once again, the All-Stars lost.

Gary sat on the bench after his teammates left,
tossing the ball between his glove and his other hand.
Coach Threads sat down beside him.
"What's bothering you, Gary?"

"I let the team down." Gary sighed. "I thought I was already a good enough third baseman, but I kept missing the ball."

"Baseball is like life," Coach Threads said. "You never stop learning or trying to be better than you were the day before. Hard work today always pays off tomorrow."

On Tuesday, Gary really wanted to go to the video game store with his friends, but instead he grabbed his glove and headed out to the field. "Hey there, Gary!" Louie the Left Fielder said. "I didn't think you were coming to the extra practices."

"If I want to be a better third baseman, I need to practice more," Gary said. Coach Threads was right. Gary needed to work harder to be his best. "Do you want to run some of those drills Coach gave us?"

"Sure!" Louie grabbed a ball and the two of them headed out past the bases. They practiced for an hour, throwing ground balls and passes, until every catch was perfect.

When the All Stars played their third game of the season, Gary was ready. He'd practiced with the team on Tuesdays and Thursdays, and also with his dad after school. As he took his place behind third base, he felt confident that he would do his best. He wasn't perfect, but he made most of his catches and throws, and in the end, the All Stars won the game, 6-4.

"Great job, Gary!" Coach Threads said. "You worked extra hard this week and it showed on the field."

Gary grinned. "The All Stars are a good baseball team," he said. "But if we all practice and work hard, we're going to be an excellent baseball team."

"Exactly." Coach Threads gave Gary a high five. The rest of the team cheered. "Now, let's all go get some celebratory ice cream cones!"

Name:

Team:

Position:

Baseball Skills on the field:

Life Skills on the field:

Threads and his Friends is a look at "Life Skills" through Baseball shared by 10 Characters representing each baseball position on the field along with the Designated Hitter. I've always believed that most "Life Skills" are easily learned with the game of baseball.

"Life Skills" such as Responsibility, Accountability, Correct Choices, Commitment, Teamwork, Hard Work, Friendship, Confidence, Honesty, and Discipline, are all part of the tools we need to give to our youth so they can grow and prosper in the game of life. As I look at our young people today, I thought these characters might be fun for them while learning "Life Skills" and some basic fundamentals at each position.

Please have fun with it!!

I would also like to thank several people who made this book possible: Lou Maggio, KR Lombardia, Gary Ippolito and Andy Taylor. Also Mario Garcia who was my Guardian Angel in this endeavor and continues to be so. A tip of the cap to all the sponsors for their financial support.

Thanks to all who have helped me on my journey.

Peter J. Mulry

Pedro
the Pitcher

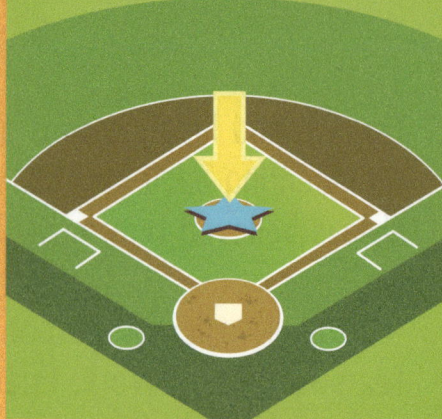

Pedro's Baseball Skills on the Field

☆ Learning how to get the right grip on a Baseball.

☆ Learning the strike zone.

☆ Learning how to get in the right position on the Pitcher's Mound.

☆ Learning wind up and proper throwing position.

☆ Learning how to pick up the Catcher's Target.

Pedro's Life Skills on the Field

Responsibility

- **Willingness** - Pay attention to coaches.
- **Acceptance** - Be a good teammate.
- **Responsive** - Pay attention to all situations in a game and be alert.
- **Talent** - Do your best and try your hardest.

Cathy
the Catcher

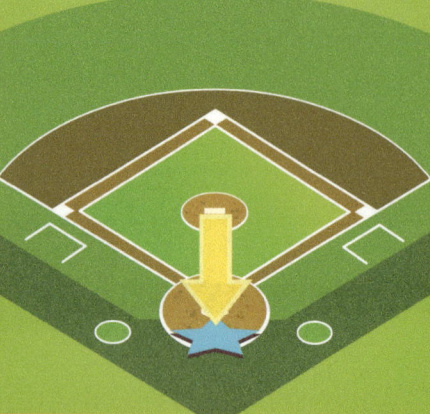

Cathy's Baseball Skills on the Field

☆ Learning how to put on the catcher's equipment.

☆ Learning the strike zone and where the target should go.

☆ Learning how to grip the ball.

☆ Telling teammates game situations and making her teammates aware of them.

Cathy's Life Skills on the Field

Accountability

Willingness - To learn the rules of how to play the game.

Accountability - Keeping herself and her teammates on the right track by being a leader.

Decision Making - Making the right choices.

Measurement - Knowing the rules. Knowing the count (balls, strikes, outs)

Freddie
the 1st Baseman

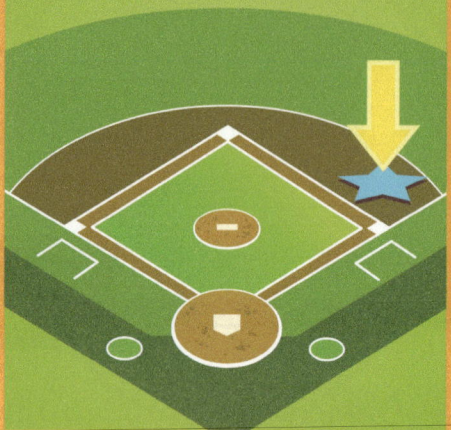

Freddie's Baseball Skills on the Field

☆ Knowing when a ground ball is hit to go to first base and put your heels on each corner of the base and be able to reach out for the ball.

☆ Learn how to use a first baseman's mitt. It will help make plays a regular glove can't—example a ball in the dirt coming from another infielder.

☆ Learning how to be the cut-off man for the balls hit to the outfield.

☆ Responsible for bunts on the right side of the field-when the situation calls for it.

Freddie's Life Skills on the Field

Correct Choices

Perception - Freddie learns by knowing what's going on every pitch during the game and what needs to be done.

Comprehension - Understand the game situation and pay attention.

Action - Taking the steps and making the choices to do what needs to be done on each play and doing it.

Manners - Know that there is a "Baseball Etiquette" when playing. "The Do's and Don'ts of the Game"

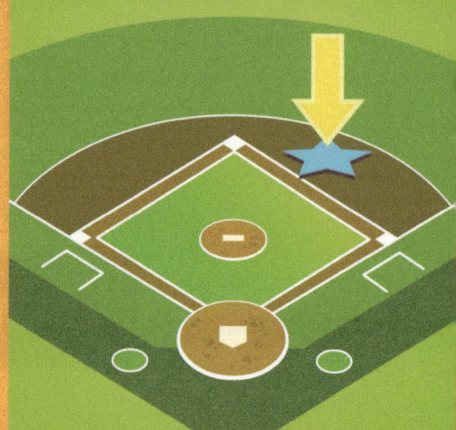

Sam
the 2nd Baseman

Sam's Baseball Skills on the Field

☆ Ground Balls hit to the 2nd baseman will go to first base.

☆ Ground balls hit to the shortstop or 3rd baseman with runners on 1st base-the 2nd baseman needs to go to second to get the throw for a force-out.

☆ In bunt plays he needs to cover first base-for the first baseman may need to field a bunt.

☆ Balls hit to the right side of the outfield—he will need to be the relay man.

Sam's Life Skills on the Field

Commitment

Conduct - Plays in a spirit of good sportsmanship.

Consistent - Belief of always giving his best on the field to himself and his team.

Sacrifice - Learning to take a little less to help one of his teammates.

Hustle - Never walk on and off the field without giving positive energy.

Samantha
the Shortstop

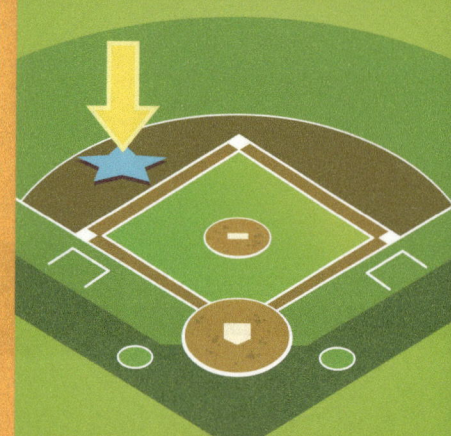

Samantha's Baseball Skills on the Field

☆ Needs the strongest throwing arm because she will make the longest throws in the infield.

☆ With a runner on first or second base and a round ball is hit to the right side she needs to cover 2nd base for a force out.

☆ In all bunt situations she needs to cover 2nd base for a possible force play.

☆ The shortstop is the relay person to the outfield from anywhere on the left side of the field.

Samantha's Life Skills on the Field

Attitude

Cooperation - She blends in with the team to get everyone to do their part. "She's a leader."

Common Goal - The common goal is to be the best we can with individuals working together to win as a team.

Respect - She knows that everyone has their own job to do and gives them encouragement to do that.

Selfless - Putting the team first-there is no "I" in team.

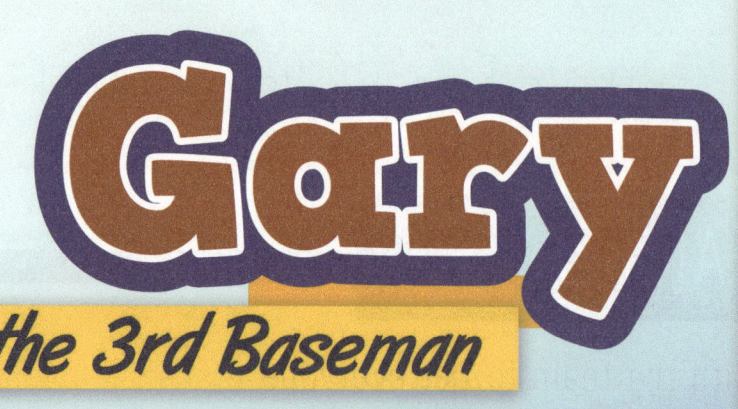
Gary
the 3rd Baseman

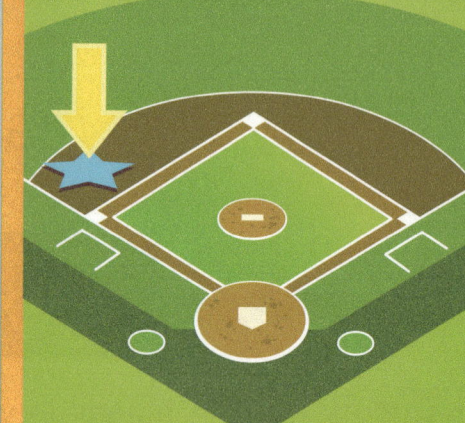

Gary's Baseball Skills on the Field

☆ The third baseman needs to have quick reactions because ground balls get to him the quickest.

☆ He needs to cover the left side on bunt plays.

☆ With a runner on first base he needs to throw to second base on ground balls for a force out.

☆ He is the relay man for balls hit into left with a runner on second base.

Gary's Life Skills on the Field

Hard Work

Discipline - Working hard every day on the field to become the best he can be. "Pay attention to the game."

Results - The end of game is determined by what you have done during the game.

Courage - Learn not to be afraid of the ball.

"Done is Never" - If you're going to be great at anything in your life you never stop working and getting better—catching ground balls every day.

Louie

the Left Fielder

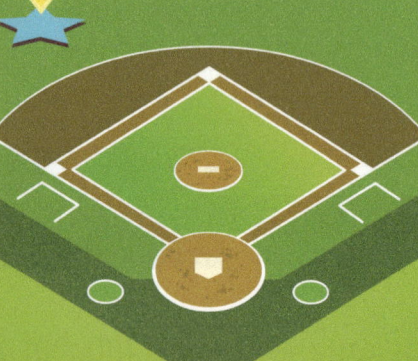

Louie's Baseball Skills on the Field

☆ Learning to catch fly balls. The best way to do this is start by using a softer ball than regular baseball.

☆ Must learn how to throw the ball a longer distance for he will make strong throws back to the infield.

☆ Needs to be taught how to long toss.

  ☆ His basic territory is from his position to the leftfield line.

  ☆ Must learn with runners on base when the ball is hit to him which base he should throw to.

Louie's Life Skills on the Field

Friendship

Trust - Trusts his coaches and teammates to do the right things and make the right decisions so his team does well.

Honesty - Being truthful to his coaches and teammates. "Louie's always honest."

Connection - Getting close to his teammates who are part of a common goal. "Lifetime contacts"

Compassion - When teammates make a mistake or a wrong play he helps them with encouraging remarks.

Chen
the Center Fielder

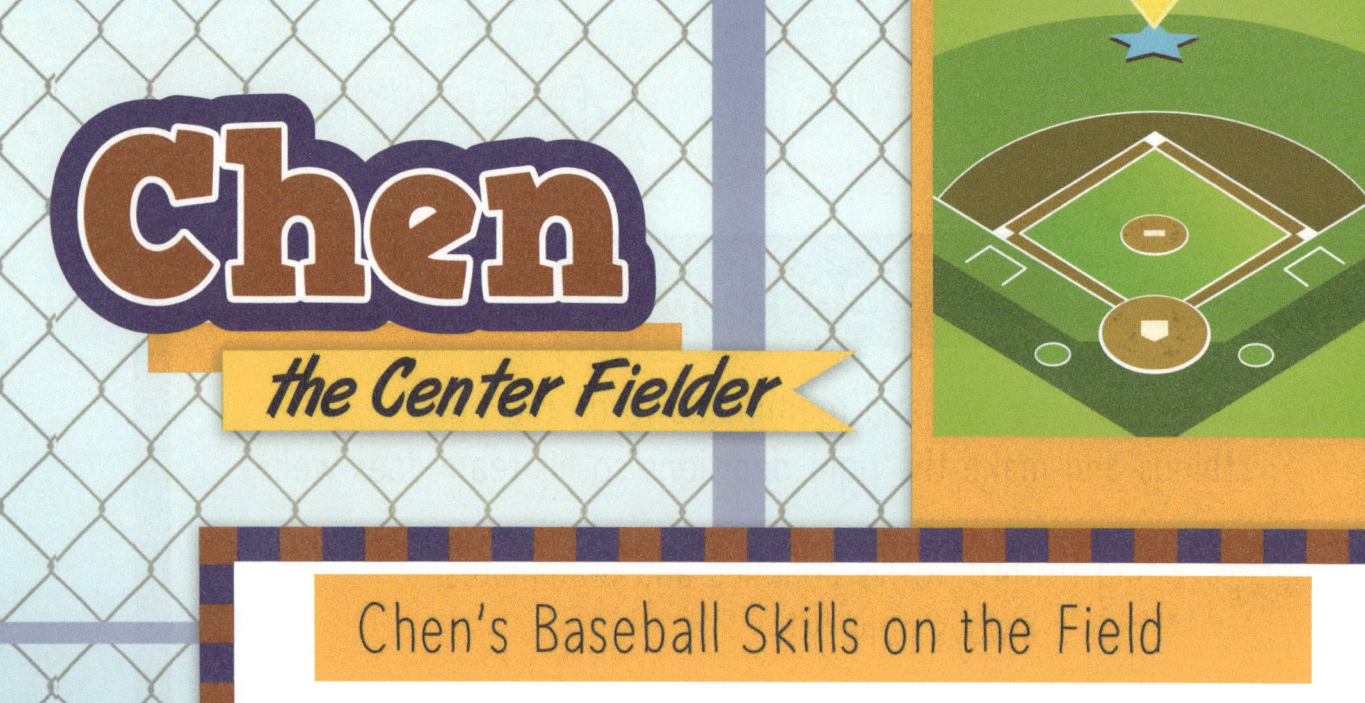

Chen's Baseball Skills on the Field

☆ Since he has the best view of the hitter he needs to get a good jump on the ball and be ready to back up his fellow outfielders.

☆ Runs to a spot where he feels the ball will be—"anticipate"

☆ Catches fly balls with his glove up. Good rule to learn is if ball is below the belly button the glove is down. If ball is above the belly button the glove is up.

☆ Knows every situation when runners are on base so he knows where the ball should go.

Chen's Life Skills on the Field

Confidence

Purpose - Always a reason for every play made on a baseball field.

Expecting - Chen wants every ball hit to him—he knows his position and everyone else on the field and knows what to do!

Tenacious - He lets everyone know in the outfield what the situation is before each pitch—he is the leader in the outfield.

Study - Always wanting to learn and get better.

Rita
the Right Fielder

Rita's Baseball Skills on the Field

☆ Don't be afraid to go to one knee when a ground ball is hit to you.

☆ Be ready to cover all the way to the right field line.

☆ Back up balls hit to the centerfielder and the first baseman.

☆ Always be ready with runners on base if the ball is hit to us—which base are we throwing to—the right fielder is usually the outfielder who has the best arm.

Rita's Life Skills on the Field

Honesty

Truth - Being honest with herself and the situations around her.

Integrity - Don't cheat to win.

Sincere - Being honest.

Be true to yourself in the game, if it doesn't feel right tell your coaches.

Tony
the Hitter

Tony's Baseball Skills on the Field

☆ Get in an athletic position with your body—feet spread apart knees bent where you're balanced and comfortable.

☆ Put the bat on your shoulder pick it up and put it back. These two steps will help get you started.

☆ Work with a batting tee (all ages) to practice your swing—you need to swing the bat every day.

☆ Learn how to follow the ball from the pitcher's hand as quickly as you can.

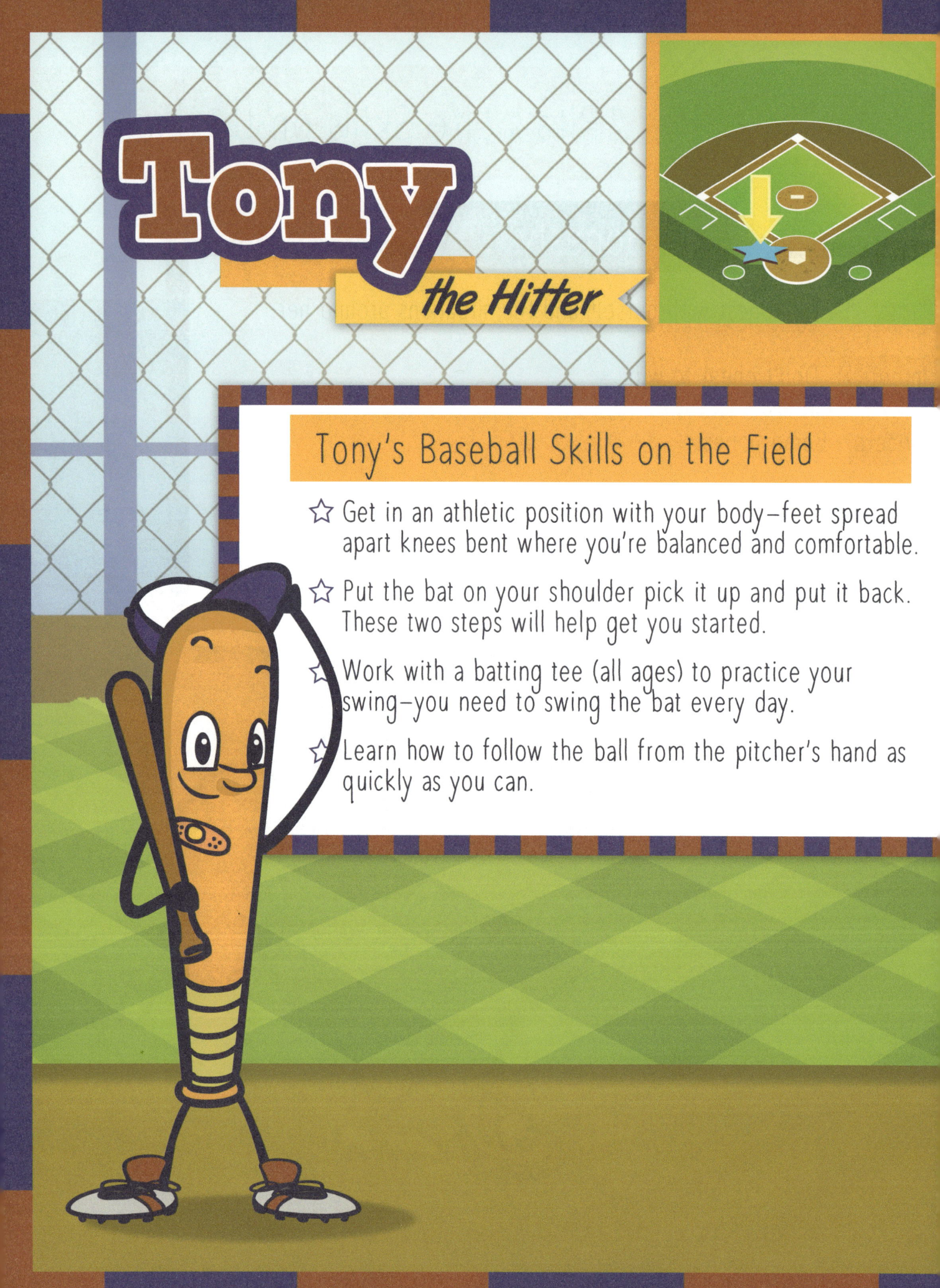

Tony's Life Skills on the Field

Discipline

Instruction - Learning to listen to coaches and instructors how to hit and get into the right hitting position.

Repetition - Learning that to be good at anything you have to do it again and again the correct way.
"Perfect practice makes perfect."

Self Control - Knowing that anything worth doing takes time and you have to have patience with yourself.
"Don't get mad."

Practice - Is the only way to get better at anything we do. However doing the right things at practice is the key.

Coach's Corner
FINANCIAL AWARENESS

Invest

In this story, Gary believed that he did not need to practice because he was the best Third Baseman. During the game, Gary kept missing plays.

He realized that when he practiced with the team he became a better player and had fun playing ball.

Investing in yourself is spending time working towards your goal.

Investing in your financial future is spending money with the goal that it will bring a profit, or more money, in the future.

How might investing help you achieve your long-term savings goal?

What examples can you think of for investing?

About the Author

Pete Mulry, one of the winningest coaches in high school baseball, coached for ten years at Tampa Catholic High School, and left that job with an overall high school record of 329-39. His team won State Championships in '68, '71, '73, and '76 and a National Championship in '73. He was honored as Florida Coach of the year in 1968, 1971, 1973 and 1976 and Nominated for National Coach of the year in 1977. Pete then moved on to the collegiate level, coaching the University of Tampa from 1978 through 1982. He also scouted for K.C. Royals. He was recently honored by the Tampa Tribune as one of the Top 50 coaches in athletics in the Tampa Bay area. He has dedicated his life, and his foundation, the Peter J. Mulry Foundation, to teach young children life skills through sports.

Look for the next book in this fun series!

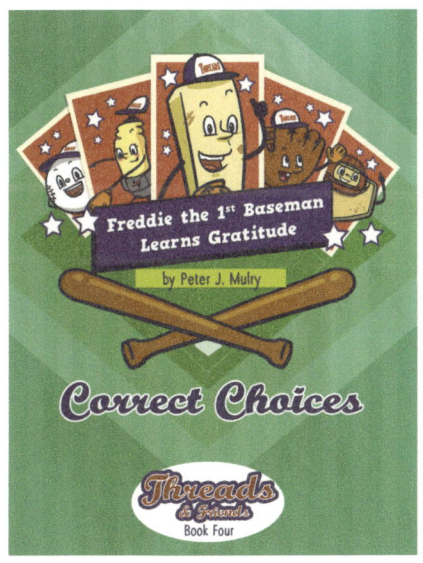

Made in the USA
Columbia, SC
15 July 2024